LIFE
IN THE
PURPLE
WEDGE

Finding Yourself on the Map and
How That Changes Everything

BY VAN HARDEN

Xulon
PRESS

LIFE IN THE PURPLE WEDGE!
Finding yourself on the map and how that changes everything.
by Van Harden

Printed in the United States of America

ISBN 9781628395105

www.xulonpress.com

CONTENTS

Chapter 1

WHERE AM I?

This book is for those for whom the times are good and joyous. It is also for those who are struggling through difficult times, problems, trials and challenges. And it is for those who feel empty. In other words, it is for anyone who has a pulse.

If you are having, or have had, those joyous times, you know how good it feels and how you would like to experience them more often. If you are struggling through tough times, you know that they are not only troubling but often also seem unfair, which only adds to the stress. And if you feel empty, maybe it is because some of those tough times have worn you down and "defeated" you. Or perhaps there is no obvious reason at all. You just feel empty.

I know I'm prejudiced, but I think this book can have huge significance in your life. This is not because it will assure you that your good and joyous circumstances will continue, or eliminate your trials, tame the cruel world, and make everything suddenly fair, or cause an emptiness you feel to leave you immediately never to come back.

However, what it *can* do is give you tremendous perspective on where you actually are right now in your life. There's nothing more grounding and assuring than knowing where you are, from where you've come, and where you are going. This kind of perspective can change everything for you. From this amazing "big picture" angle, you'll find that your life and daily routine look very different from the view you are seeing in your up-close, daily look at the detail and minutia with which you are bombarded. Most people think they know where they are—if not consciously then subconsciously. I'm convinced most don't. I know I didn't.

I have no intention of sounding arrogant, as though I know something no one else knows.

What I am presenting here are things that many have known for a long time. In fact, you probably already know a lot of what I'm going to tell you. It's just that these things have been out there as puzzle pieces, and, at least for me, no one did a very good job of piecing them together in a way that I could truly say, "Oh, I get it!" I hope this book will do that for you. I'm even going to draw some illustrations to help. If you're still with me, you are way ahead of many others.

Some see all these puzzle pieces in their lives and don't even know they are designed to somehow fit together. Others see the pieces and realize what they are, but they never try to put them together, perhaps because that task seems so overwhelming. Then there are those who are constantly trying to put them together but are continually frustrated.

Have you ever been to a new or unfamiliar shopping mall and suddenly realized you didn't know exactly where you were? Or maybe you thought you did, only to find out you didn't. Life is like that. Sometimes we feel totally lost. Sometimes we think we know where we are, but we are not confident. Sometimes we are absolutely certain we know where we are, whether we are right or wrong.

At the mall they spend big bucks on back-lit, multicolored display maps of the mall's layout, showing every store on every floor. As you stop and look at one of these displays, what is the one thing that helps you most? Exactly! It's the "You are Here!" marker. The entire map is nice, but without the marker "You are Here," it's only an expensive, nicely done portrait of a building. It leaves out the most important part: you! After seeing that mark, you get your bearings. It changes things for you. Suddenly you have perspective.

Whether this book is a major revelation to you, a helpful tool in putting together the pieces you knew were there, or just an interesting read, one thing we know for sure: everybody has to be somewhere. Is it possible you are somewhere you didn't fully realize? Let's explore.

Chapter 2

THE COMPLICATED LITTLE
RED CIRCLE

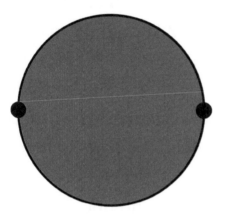

The first part of your map is a simple little circle. Let's make it red. Red is a very vibrant, fun, yet fiery color, representative of the ups and downs of life. The extreme left edge of the circle is the day you were born, indicated with a dot. The extreme right edge is the day you will die, also shown as a dot. You had absolutely no control over the timing of the left edge of the circle—or that there is a circle at all. The vast majority of people do not control the right edge either. We'll touch more on that later. Other people take care of us on the early left side of the red circle. That is also happening with more frequency on the far right side.

Somewhere in that red circle you could make a star or a dot and write, "I am here." Where would you put the star? You could make an educated guess, but you don't really know for sure. It's a bit like being at that unfamiliar mall, standing in front of that expensive locator map but finding they haven't added the "you are here" star to give you perspective. Generally you know where you are; specifically you do not.

As you know, the red circle can be a wild ride, with circumstances ranging from perfection to disaster and emotions fluctuating from ecstasy to depression. This is the only world in which we've lived. While on the surface of the moon, one of the Apollo astronauts mentioned that as he stopped his work and looked back at the earth, it was very odd to be able to hold his thumb up on his outstretched hand and cover up everything he had ever known. Everything we've learned, we've learned here. Everything we've ever known, we've known from here. If we had come here from some other planet or world, we would have something to which we could compare this life. We didn't, and we don't.

I'm stating the elementary here for a reason. The fact that it is so elementary and so obvious is the very reason so many of us miss anything beyond that. We are stuck on the obvious of this world, and it so fills our minds and our beings that there is little room for anything else, even if that "obvious" is merely a small part of life and what is real. We are consumed by the red circle. We think about it constantly. The red circle is complicated for sure. It weighs on us and drives us to do the things we do.

However, remember that I also described the circle as "little." It doesn't seem little, does it? It seems like everything. Yet, in truth, the circle is so little that it is dwarfed by the rest of the map! Even if you could magically know exactly where to draw your star in the red circle, you still wouldn't know where you are. That's because there is so much more to the map. We're taking this one step at a time. The complicated little red circle was step one. Before we move on to the other parts of the map, let's look at some very surprising descriptions and explanations of this red circle in which you live, given by people with very impressive credentials.

Chapter 3

YOUR WORLD, YOUR SITUATIONS

How's your world right now? How's your life? How's your red circle going? It's amazing how many people, when asked, "How's it going?" or "How are you?" will say, "Fine," whether that's true or not. And if you're the one being asked, you might wonder sometimes whether the inquirer really wants a true answer or is simply making small talk.

With so many circumstances and emotions in life, both good and bad, there obviously are many true answers to the question, depending upon who is being asked, but you would have to be living in a cave not to have heard all the problems, anguish, and despair many people are having and feeling these days. We all have heard, and maybe even experienced, problems with health, relationships, money, depression, worries, deaths, political concerns, family, world and national scares, divorce, unemployment, jobs themselves, children, crime, and lack of self-worth. Those challenges just scratch the surface. You know your own concerns all too well.

Even with its many joys and gifts, this world can be very rough, trying, frightening, and exhausting. If your experience makes you feel like an expert on that topic, you're not alone. In fact, you're in extremely good company. And to verify how right you are, consider the following statements about the world in which you and I live from someone with some extremely high credentials — namely, Jesus.

- "In this world you will have trouble." (John 17:33b)
- "Do not lay up for yourselves treasures upon earth, where moths and rust destroy, and where thieves break in and steal." (Matthew 6:19 NASB)

- "Now judgment is upon this world." (John 12:31 NASB)

There are other words of Jesus that seem very derogatory toward the red circle in which we live. When I first studied those quotes, I was a bit surprised and even a bit disheartened. After all, doesn't the Bible say that God Himself saw that "it was good," or even "very good," after each of the six days of creation? But since Jesus Himself later talks about what a troubled place this is now, where is the hope and joy we all desire and that would seem to be associated with a loving God? If Jesus says the red circle is full of evil, how can I have any encouragement at all for my life, since the red circle is where I live? That indeed seems depressing.

Some have come to the conclusion that we, as individuals and as a society, have to be good and work our way to peace and happiness and that only then will life in the red circle be good. Others believe that life in the red circle will never be truly good and that we'll just have to put up with the junk in this world, hope time goes by quickly, and then—if we are believers—be rewarded when we go to heaven. Others believe you live, you die, and that's all. I'm convinced all three of these perspectives are shortsighted.

The condemning of "this world" certainly is not exclusive to Jesus. In his red circle world, King Solomon, often called the wisest man who ever lived, tried every pleasure he could afford, and he could afford them all. He left us with his famous conclusion: "Vanity of vanities! All is vanity!" (Ecclesiastes 1:2). It wasn't so much that Solomon was unhappy with the bad. Rather, as often is the case for us in this world, he wasn't satisfied with the good. His red circle was completely filled with material "good," yet for him that "good" just wasn't good enough.

Paul also had some things to say about life in the red circle.

- "Do not be conformed to this world." (Romans 12:2 NASB)
- "For the wisdom of this world is foolishness in God's sight." (1 Corinthians 3:19)

- "See to it that no one takes you captive through hollow and deceptive philosophy which depends upon human tradition and the basic principals of this world rather than on Christ." (Colossians 2:8)

This world! This world! This world! Over and over we hear about "this world." But there is a simple clue in that phrase. If there is a "this world," there must be a "that world!" There must be another world!

Forever people have been preaching that when we die we will go to heaven, to another world. And there is no doubt among believers that the so-called "afterlife" will be another world. On the big mall directory map of our life, the drawing of "that world" seemingly would begin immediately where "this world," the red circle, ends for a person; that is, when the person dies. *Seemingly*—but such a map would not be accurate.

The more you look at this and study it, the more you can see there is more to it than that. For believers, there is much more to existence than simply passing out of one world and into another. As I spent time with this, I got excited because the way the pieces fit together seems to provide a beautiful answer to so much of the discomfort, trial, and tribulation of the red circle.

Chapter 4

"THAT" WORLD

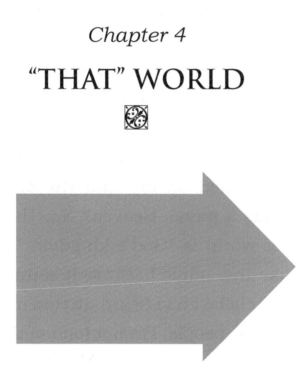

So this world is the small red circle with your birth on the left side and your death on the right. And from personal experience, as well as from the teaching of Jesus, Paul and others, both spiritual and nonspiritual, we know the hardships, difficulties, and unfairness this world presents to us. We are in the midst of it. We are living it. We will return to talk about this world, but for now, let's tuck that away and move on to what would seem to be its opposite, the other world.

In thinking about this other world, I grappled with two things. For clarity, what should I call this other world? And what design could I use as an illustration? The red circle was appropriate for this world, but what about that other world? I agonized for a name, but none seemed adequate. Then it dawned on me that the other world already has a name. Heaven? No. The name of the other world is "God's kingdom." At first, I didn't like this name because it sounded like a "religious" cliché I had heard uttered many times by "religious" people. I'm not fond of things that sound especially "religious." The Pharisees were especially religious, and I have no desire to be a Pharisee. But I do have a desire to know the truth and to be whatever God wants me to be. It doesn't really matter what you or I think about things that sound "religious." What matters is what is true. The kingdom of God is true. If I don't like that term, I'll just have to get over it.

God's kingdom is so totally different from this world, it would have to be represented by a totally different color. I chose blue. Unlike the small red circle, this illustration would have to be huge. How would I draw a huge, blue, unending presence that has infinite height and width? I decided to draw a line down the center of a page with absolutely everything to its right in blue. But it must be understood that the blue color is infinite to the right of that line and both up and down. Keep that in mind whenever you see the blue illustration.

Am I sure that's not heaven? Yes. Everyone in heaven is in God's kingdom. They are in the 100 percent blue portion of the map. But not everyone in God's kingdom is in heaven. Is it really possible to live in two worlds at the same time? Absolutely! If you are a Christian, you already are! There comes a point where two worlds collide. I'm guessing many of you reading this have already felt the collision and continue to feel it everyday. When a person lives in the red world only and then becomes a Christian, God slides His gigantic, perfect, never-ending, blue kingdom over the right portion of the red world in which that person is living. So if that's you, your red world turns bluer and your new blue world turns redder. Welcome to life in the purple wedge! All of a sudden, the map of your life and your world becomes huge and unending. That is indeed a big change! You have both feet in both worlds at the same time, at least for now. An understanding of this may or may not change what happens to you in this world, but it will definitely change how you see, react to, and handle things, especially if you keep in mind the new knowledge you have of where you are. And that can definitely change some things for the better during your stay in the red circle.

Chapter 5

BEING IN THE WEDGE

We're creeping closer to putting your star on the map to identify where you are. If you've been a Christian since childhood, the gigantic blue part of the map covers much of your red circle. There is a lot of purple on your map since the blue overlapped the red relatively early in your life, near the left side of your red circle. As seen in figure A, that's the biggest, longest kind of purple wedge.

If you became a Christian in what would seem to be midlife, the left half of your circle is red and the right half is

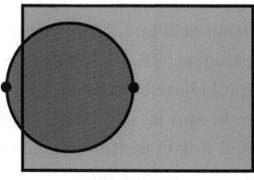

Figure A

covered by the blue of God's kingdom, thus making that right half purple, as seen in figure B.

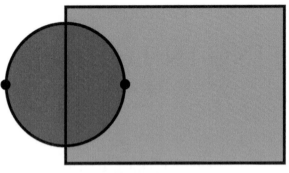

Figure B

And if you became a Christian late in life, as in figure C, most of your circle is red, but a portion on the right side is purple since the blue covering made it that way. Who would have a map that looked like that? As an extreme example, think of one of the thieves on the cross. It appears he surrendered to Christ on the last day of his life, probably even the last few hours. Jesus told him, "This day you will be with me in paradise." That being the case, his purple wedge would have been just a small sliver, yet that thief was, and is, in God's kingdom. Someone who had a true deathbed conversion would have a similar-looking map.

24

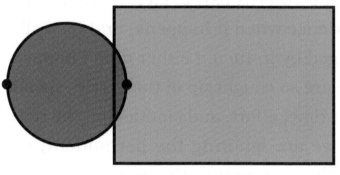

Figure C

You do not have to die to enter God's kingdom. At times things seem so difficult for some believers that they wish Jesus would return immediately or even that they might die. We all know of cases where people have acted on these feelings by taking their own lives. But I repeat, you do not have to die to enter God's kingdom!

It is a shame that so many Christians do not realize, believe, understand, remember, or at least act as though they immediately entered God's kingdom when they surrendered to God, through Christ, the way God instructs. What an honor it is that God moved His big, blue eternity over the final part of our red circle. He didn't have to do that. None of us is good enough to deserve it. It is an undeserved gift, with absolutely no obligation on His part to give. It is a life-changing experience when it happens, and if our life isn't changed by it, then it either didn't happen at all or we are so caught up in this world, spending so much time, effort, and emotion on the red circle, that we are ignoring the permanent, eternal, gigantic, blue part of the map in which we will forever be.

If you are a Christian, especially if you are unhappy or frustrated, remind yourself frequently of the purple wedge in which you live. Draw out your own picture of it, or use one in this book. Take it with you. Put it in your wallet or purse. Put one on your refrigerator door. Put it on your desk and next to your bed. Surround yourself with this reminder of who and where you are!

While staring at your map, look to the left of the purple wedge. You already know all too well from personal experience—and Jesus and Paul agreed—there is much junk, unfairness, pain, frustration, hurt, and evil in that red circle. This is the place from which you came. If your mind dwells on this red-circle world and the garbage it may be throwing your way, you are returning there. DO NOT GO BACK! You have been there once. You've already been through that, and you are done with it. Through Christ you are victorious over all that! Your world is now purple, and someday—and it could be soon—it will be totally blue. Look to the right side of your map, not to the left! If you go back, you will go back with a frown. If you realize where you are and look forward, you will move on with a smile. Even though the red part of the purple wedge will still throw hurts, challenges, disappointments, anger, unfairness, and other emotional things at you, you will have a joy that this red world will never be able to take away. Look to the blue, not the red, and be thankful for the purple!

Chapter 6

TRYING SO HARD

W̲e are conditioned to try very hard to make our lives and our world what we want them to be. A lot of what we want in this world is admirable: weight loss, better relationships, and politicians who are on our side. We like and want things to spruce up our red circle and make us feel good, and we are pretty sure we know what those things should be.

My grandfather was a huge fan of the University of Nebraska football team. I remember being at his house one time when the Cornhuskers were playing on TV. He was riveted to every play. I noticed that as he watched, he wasn't sitting up straight in the chair. He was leaning to the left. I thought maybe he was going to fall asleep, but then I realized there was no way that was going to happen when he was so passionate about his team and the game.

Later in the game I noticed he was leaning again but this time to the right! I finally figured out that he was subconsciously "helping" his team. Whichever way they were marching down the field on the TV screen, that was the direction in which he leaned. That game got so close, I thought he was going to fall onto the floor! When we made fun of him, he laughed too; but he honestly didn't realize he was doing it.

We could all laugh at him as much as we wanted, but the fact is that we humans in the red circle emotionally, intellectually, physically, and physiologically almost always lean toward what we want to happen and what we want to be true, even if it won't happen and isn't true. If you look at the world's religions and then list them in order, according to each one's number of adherents, it might make for an interesting discussion; but I would argue that the largest denomination in the world will never be listed or even acknowledged. That's because I contend that the largest religion in the world is "The Gospel According to What I Want to be True."

In this denomination you will find people of every faith and non-faith. On any particular issue, many people, no matter what group they are in, will lean in the direction they want to be true, whether it is or not. Many think truth can be whatever they want it to be, and once they have made up their minds as to that truth, there's no turning back, because that would be an admission that they had been ... ugh ... wrong!

I did not make up the red circle, the purple wedge, or the blue eternity. I noticed them. There was a time when I was riding through life, leaning toward whichever way I wanted life and all its details to go. That was red-circle living for this world.

When I started studying the Bible, I felt pretty good about myself and what I was doing. After all, what could be more virtuous than studying the Bible? I read a lot of things I wholeheartedly agreed with, and I even subconsciously cheered God for His stand and His actions. I was leaning in the same direction He was, marching down the field.

But the more I studied and the more I lived in the red circle, and even in the purple wedge, the more frequently I encountered things God either caused or allowed that I didn't like and that just didn't seem right to me. And I asked the same questions people ask Him every day: "God, how could You allow that to happen? How is it possible that a perfect God like You would work this way? God, this does not seem right. I would never do it this way if I were You!"

I read in the Bible that I was supposed to rejoice in everything and even give thanks for my trials and tribulations. "Oh, come on God! Surely You are wise enough to know that's not normal, practical, or even possible." So in one part of my Bible study, I was cheering; yet in others I was troubled, disagreeing with God, and even avoiding certain issues. Why? Because I was living by the gospel according to the way I wanted things to be. That gospel is epidemic in this world, the little red circle. Unfortunately, it is even rampant in the purple wedge.

It struck me hard that when I read and studied the Bible, I started with my own preconceived notions, prejudices, and ideas of truth. I wasn't really looking for truth. I was looking for God's confirmation of mine. Many times I got it. But over and over I ran into these nagging notions of the Bible that I really didn't like. For some reason, the image of Grandpa leaning in his chair came to mind, for I was doing much the same thing.

This all led to big questions I knew I had to answer. "Van, are you going to believe this book or not? Will you read and study only the parts you like and ignore the parts you don't? Are you really a Christian? Is the Bible totally true, partially true, or maybe not true at all?" It cut so deeply into my heart that I considered dropping the Bible altogether as a part of my life. I did not want to be a hypocrite, promoting the Bible on one occasion but not on another.

Then two more questions came to me. The first was, "Do you believe in God?" My immediate answer was, "Yes." The other question was, "Who is smarter, you or God?" My knee-jerk answer was that most of the time He was. Then I realized what a stupid, worldly, arrogant, prideful, small, red-circle, selfish answer that was. And I vividly remember making the decision then that I would believe God's Word, even if I would do things differently than He does. Thank God, I do believe and cherish His Word, even when it is hard and unpopular. Now, instead of opening up the Bible to parts I know I'll like, I study it all. And I sit straight up in my chair.

Trying so hard to make things go our way in this world, doing so much leaning, is exhausting. I am convinced that is exactly what Jesus had in mind when He said, "Come to me all you who are weary and heavy-laden and I will give you rest" (Matthew 11:28 NASB). Look at your map. Realize where you are. The weariness and burden is in the red section on the left. If you're like me, you've had enough of that. Focus and dwell upon the right side of that map. Bask in the purple and blue!

Chapter 7

THE RULERS OF THE WORLDS

Our God can, will, and does do anything He wants whenever He wants. Another way of saying that is that God is sovereign. What a huge effect this has on every day, even every moment of life. We frequently spend years, sometimes even a lifetime, resisting and fighting this, since, as I've pointed out about myself, God does things many of us would never do. And even the things He does that please us are often done in a way we would never have thought of, let alone actually done. All this is a good preface for looking at the rulers of "this" red world and "that" blue world.

Who rules this earth on which we live? I always assumed that since God created planet Earth, He ruled over it. But consider Jesus' comments about someone He called, "The ruler of this world" (John 12:31 NASB), in which He was clearly not talking about Himself. Ephesians 2:2 talks about "when you followed the ways of this world and the ruler of the kingdom of the air." And 1 John 5:19 mentions that "the whole world is under the control of the evil one." That should get everyone's attention! This world in which you live and dwell every moment of every day is ruled by someone Jesus called "the evil one." But this is not out of God's control. He allows it.

Who is the evil one? And will he be defeated? In describing the end times of the earth, Revelation 20:2 identifies the ruler of this world in four different ways, so we know for sure who it is. He is called, "the dragon, the ancient serpent, who is the devil, or Satan." If it had not been Jesus Himself telling us about this, I would find this very hard to believe. In fact, I still find it difficult to think that our loving, infinitely wise God would let Satan, the devil, rule over the world in which we live. If you were God, would you allow that? If I were God, that would be about the last thing I would allow, or even consider. Sometimes

I think I'd make a pretty good God. But everyone is fortunate I am not God. "For my thoughts are not your thoughts, neither are your ways my ways" (Isaiah 55:8). And whether I like it or not, Satan is the ruler of this world.

Look at your map and at everything that is red. Satan rules there. That knowledge should have a profound effect on your life and the decisions you make. He may be the ruler of "this world," but he does not have to be the ruler of your life! In fact, a big part of this whole "this world/that world" issue is the question, "Who will be your ruler?" Satan does not care about you. He cares only about himself. And the only real reason he would be interested in you is to use you for his benefit.

For God's own reasons (which have to be good since He is God), He chooses to permit Satan to be the ruler of this world, at least for a while. God is sovereign and could end Satan's rule at any minute, and one day He will. But meanwhile, we who are living in this world are to choose our ruler. Satan is being permitted to reign over the little red circle, and there seems to be two ways we can choose him. We can choose him directly, which a few do; or we can choose his rule indirectly by choosing ourselves as our ruler, as so many do.

And who is the ruler of God's blue, eternal, never-ending kingdom? Consider a few verses. "Then Jesus came to them and said, 'All authority in heaven and earth has been given to Me'" (Matthew 28:18). Colossians 1:16-17 also speaks about Jesus, saying, "For by him all things were created: things in heaven and on earth, visible and invisible, whether thrones or powers or rulers or authorities; all things were created by and for him. He is before all things, and in him all things hold together."

So whom do you choose as your ruler: Satan, yourself, or Jesus? It seems like a no-brainer, yet we are so into ourselves and this little red temporary world and all the distractions of life, that even when we choose Jesus and start living in the purple wedge, we tend to put Him and His kingdom way down on our priority list. Have you ever had a time in your life when things didn't seem to be holding together very well? I have. I really believe that verse that says "in him all things hold together," because in those times when they weren't holding together, I seemed to be farthest from Him. He hadn't moved. I had. If, in Him all things hold together, why would anyone ever want to be apart from Him?

So there you have the rulers of the red and the blue worlds. For many of you, God put something in you to side with Christ. For many others of you, He may be doing that for you right now. The big question for believers is this: Will we continue to choose Him daily, and even moment by moment, or will we be so pulled and affected by this world and its emotions that we won't get out of the red?

Chapter 8

THE DILEMMA OF THE PURPLE WEDGE

Peple who have become Christians, and therefore live in the purple wedge, sometimes feel frustrated, not only with "this world" but also with themselves. Let's explore two examples and see if either of these sounds familiar.

First of all, since God is perfect and you are now one with Him through His Son, shouldn't you be in line for more blessings and happiness in life here in this world? Wouldn't that seem to make sense? There are a lot of "evangelists" out there preaching and teaching how much better things are going to be for you in terms of money, relationships, jobs, etc. when you come to Christ. That has been labeled by some as the "prosperity gospel." Some Christians actually do prosper materially and physically, yet the truth is that often, after becoming Christians, people do not receive more of the wants on their lists. In fact, they might actually face more frustrating earthly challenges and even persecution. They might begin to think that this purple wedge stuff stinks and that they were better off totally in the little red circle.

That way of thinking assumes one thing, and I'm just going to say it bluntly here. It assumes, probably subconsciously, that you are really God and the purpose of life is to please you. But the entire conversion to Christ and life in the purple wedge is the point at which that way of thinking ends with your waving the white flag and totally surrendering your life to God through Jesus.

Life's purpose is entirely different to you in the purple wedge than it was in the red circle. Success is no longer defined by your getting what you want but by God getting what He wants. Good and bad are no longer defined by what you think but rather by what He thinks. No longer are the opinions of which you've been so convicted as important as God's opinions. In moving from the red circle to the purple wedge, there has been a major shift! The fastest, clearest, and most concise way I can put it is like this: the foundation of your life has shifted from *me* to *He*. If you do not see such a shift, you have serious reason to question whether you really did pass from the red circle to the purple wedge. For whom do you live?

Remember, with life in the purple wedge, you still are partially in the red circle with all its frustrating and even heartbreaking evils. But now, since you are also in God's kingdom, you have a whole new way to look at these things. Your perspective has changed. If something frustrating happens to you, you know that God, for His own perfect reasons, either caused it or allowed it. And even if you're not entirely pleased that He did it or allowed it, you know that all things work together for His glory, even if you tend to think it doesn't work for yours. The fact is, if God wins, you win; so stick with Him closely through thick and thin.

Many Christians become frustrated with themselves. They know all the things of which I just spoke, yet they do not live that way. Many want to live and think the way they know God wants them to, but they just keep falling back into red-circle thinking and living. There was a man who experienced this and was so frustrated by it that he wrote about it. Here is what he had to say. "I do not understand what I do. For what I want to do I do not do, but what I hate, I do." He didn't say he hated himself, but it sounds like maybe that's what he was getting at. Many people do hate themselves when this happens.

The man who wrote that was a believer. The man who wrote that was living in the purple wedge. The man who wrote that was one of the greatest saints who ever walked the earth. The man who wrote that was the apostle Paul (Romans 7:15-16). Paul was not just casually mentioning this. He was consumed, frustrated, and in desperation about his worldly thoughts and actions. He knew he had already entered God's kingdom, but that stood in contrast to some of the things he said and did.

This dilemma of self-disappointment faces those of us living in the purple wedge. What's the answer to this one? Well, the guy who found and stated the problem also found and stated the answer for us all: "What a wretched man I am! Who will rescue me from this body of death? Thanks be to God – through Jesus Christ our Lord!" (Romans 7: 24-25). As with the previous problem, the answer is a personal shift of surrender from *me* to *He*. No one has ever been perfect at that. No one has even been close—not even Paul. But Paul and many others asked God to pick them up again so they could carry on in the purple wedge. God did, and He does. That is extremely encouraging for you and me, and it is important to remember *when*—not *if*—we fall.

We'll never be perfect in ourselves, but with God we can always get much better. Maybe you've heard the song about Him washing us whiter than snow. We are not perfect in ourselves, but in Him we are. In the red circle of this world, there is no hope. However, because you're living in the purple wedge, there is always His hope, power, and joy.

Chapter 9

THE JOY OF THE PURPLE WEDGE

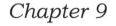

While dilemmas are many for those living in the purple wedge, joys are far more. Worldly, red-circle problems, challenges, cares, and worries may hammer and pound you day and night. That's not unusual. That's part of the enemy's plan as the ruler of this world. His goal is to keep your heart and mind off God and His kingdom. We seem to fall for that daily, without realizing it or thinking about it. However, there are incredibly positive aspects of life in the purple wedge that we need to talk about.

One of the most freeing, satisfying, liberating joys in life is realizing from where you came, who you really are, and where you're going; hence the map we've been drawing. I started out by saying that I was convinced most people do not realize who or where they are, even though they think they do. The red, purple, and blue help us to identify where we are. We know we are in the red circle; and if we are Christians, we should know that we are in the purple wedge part of that red circle. And we know why it is purple: because God's kingdom took over our lives even though we are still living here on earth and this world is still having an effect on us. We also know that the blue part of the map, which is 100 percent God's kingdom, is next for us. With that comes the promise of never, ever being separated from God. We may not know exactly where the "You are here" mark goes in the purple wedge, because we don't know when we will die physically; but we know we are there, how we arrived, and where we are going next. When you look at that map, you should feel secure and honored that God loves you so much! That knowledge is a joy and a privilege. No one can ever take that from you because no one can ever take you from God!

Another joy is that when you live in the purple wedge ordinary things look different than they used to. In fact, many times they no longer look ordinary at all. What a joy it is to look at loved ones, flowers, trees, the sky, birds, mountains, babies, and sunsets, to mention a very few things, and know how special they really are. What a joy it is to see the hand of God around you constantly, even in a troubled world.

What a joy it is to know that since you have entered the purple wedge you have continual access to God and that will never change. He wants your fellowship. He wants you to talk to Him through prayer. No matter where you are—on top of a mountain, buried deep in a mine, walking on Mars, or anywhere else—you can get in touch with Him immediately, and the line will never be busy. He wants your adoration. He wants your confessions. He wants your thankfulness. He wants your requests. But most of all, He wants you and your love for Him with all your heart, strength, mind, and soul. What a joy it is to be so wanted by the Creator of everything.

There are probably many Christians who just don't feel this way, and that is sad; but what a joy and honor it is to teach people about the tremendous love of God and the plan He has for them. I've heard it said many times when talking about going to heaven, "You can't take it with you." It's true that you cannot take with you your house, car, money, or other things you have valued here on earth, but how about your husband, wife, parents, children, friends, and acquaintances? You personally will never be able to get someone into heaven, but God certainly can use you as a tool to spread the good news as He brings more people to Himself. He would love to have you plant some seeds for Him. What an amazing thing it would be if He watered and grew just one of those seeds you planted and a person came to Him through you.

Does this sound intimidating? It would be if you had to be a Bible scholar with a long, practiced presentation in order to tell the story to others. But all you really need is the fortitude to tell people your own story of what God has done for you. People will argue with Bible scholars. They can't argue with your own personal story. There is only one expert in the world on that topic: you! For whatever reason, God must have had *life in the purple wedge* pop into my heart, my mind, and my pen. I have found the concept helpful in my own life, and other people seem to latch onto it, so I use it to witness.

Counting and listing the joys of life in the purple wedge would be an endless task, but let me mention just one more thing that has been incredibly important to me. Just as a little child seems content and safe in the arms of his or her mother, I feel as though I am being wrapped in God's arms in this life in the purple wedge. No matter how smart, strong, macho, independent, or old we feel, and no matter what the red circle throws at us, our inner beings long for that wrapping. In the purple wedge we have it, whether we've yet learned to accept it and feel it or not. What a joy it is to fully realize that great truth!

Chapter 10

YOUR BIG "X"

W e are frequently trying to "fix" ourselves. One of the things that frustrates us in "this" world is the way we look and feel. Everybody wants to looks better. Everybody wants to feel better. And we can't blame a person for that! We are frequently dissatisfied with our bodies and how they look and work. Plastic surgeons, weight-loss businesses, hip and knee replacers, fitness centers, laser vision doctors, teeth whiteners and straighteners, energy drinks, prescription drugs, nonprescription drugs, and hearing specialists are in great demand, and a multitude of "improvers" are making a fortune these days.

To our credit, we are using many of these things so we can be the best we can be. To our detriment, we overuse, misuse, and even abuse most of them. Why? Because the human body, in this red world, deteriorates. I've never heard anyone say, "Please don't talk so loud. My hearing is much better than it used to be"; or, "I threw my reading glasses away since my eyesight has gotten so much stronger"; or, "It's great to have twice the energy I had when I was young!" If we'd been born old, and got younger, maybe we would hear some of those things, but we all know that's not the way it works.

If we were to draw a line graph of the overall fitness of our body over time, including all its parts and functions, it would be trending lower

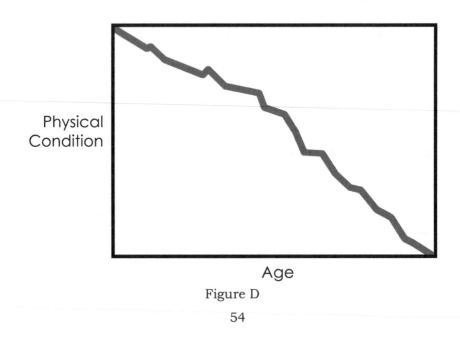

Figure D

all the time, as in figure D. Some people's lines would drop slower than others, and some may even have an occasional, brief uptick, perhaps due to utilizing some of those things mentioned above. But, in the long run, everybody's line would trend downward. And, other than Christ, no one has been able to overcome the fact that eventually the body dies. That's all normal. Physically we deteriorate. That is the earthly, red-circle part of us.

Compare that to the spiritual part of our lives, represented by the purple and blue areas. If we drew a line graph for our spiritual fitness, it

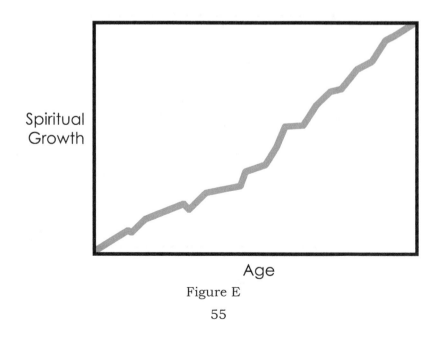

Figure E

would start at the bottom and work its way up, unlike the physical fitness graph, which starts high up on the chart and works its way down. Normally our faith and spiritual wisdom grow as we get older, because we are investing more and more time in reading, study, prayer, fellowship, and worship, as in figure E.

So, imagine superimposing one line graph over the other. The physical fitness line starts high and goes down. The spiritual fitness line starts low and goes up. Eventually these two lines of your life cross one another. If you were to look at a mature Christian's chart at the end

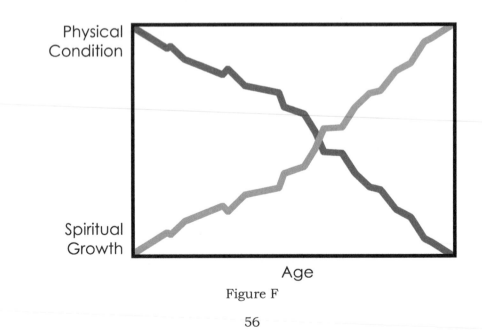

Figure F

of his or her life, you would see a big *X,* as in figure F. No matter what they tell you on the infomercials, it is impossible for a physical life to get better and better, but that is not true of a Christian's spiritual life. Spiritual life defies death. Paul had several things to say about spiritual growth.

> Let your roots grow down into Him, and let your lives be built on Him. There your faith will grow strong in the truth you were taught and you will overflow with thankfulness.
> Colossians 2:7-8

> Our hope is that, as your faith continues to grow, our area of activity among you will greatly expand.
> 2 Corinthians 10:15

What a revelation and blessing it has been for me to see these puzzle pieces put together. As a visual learner, it helps give me perspective on who and where I am and what is happening to me physically and spiritually.

So the next time you are frustrated because you can't find your reading glasses, or you have to take pills, or you don't have the energy you used to have, or you have some other frustration that reminds you of life's physical deterioration, rejoice in the fact that as a Christian living in the purple wedge, you can get better and stronger spiritually right down to your last physical breath—and beyond. I've heard people trying to console others on their birthdays, either in sarcasm or sincerity, saying, "Hey, you're not getting older; you're getting better." Growing believers should rejoice, for spiritually they are indeed getting better!

Chapter 11

PASSING INTO THE BLUE

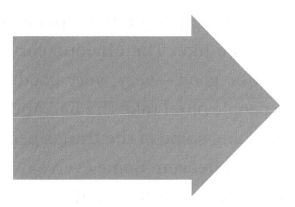

As mentioned earlier about the red-circle map, the day you were born would be on the far left side of the circle. On the far right side is the day you will die physically. That's true whether you are a Christian believer or not. I mentioned too that when you become a believer, you enter God's kingdom, even though you are still in this world. God's blue kingdom overlaps that part of your red circle that still remains before you die. Therefore, you live in two worlds at the same time, and thus in "the purple wedge." It is a joyous honor to pass from the red circle into the purple wedge.

But those who live in the purple wedge will one day pass into the 100 percent blue kingdom of God. What is that blue kingdom like? For a long, long time people have pondered what heaven will be like. The obvious consensus is that it will be good—very, very good. But that is where people often take the ball and run with it. It is amazing some of the things people think and say about heaven. Some even say they have been there and returned, and then they write books about it. Although scripturally I find that hard to believe, I know that God can, will, and does do whatever He pleases, so I don't discount the possibility.

Our life experience has been confined to this earth. Thus, in thinking about what that blue, heavenly kingdom will be like, our finite minds gravitate to the absolute "best" things and emotions we have encountered here. We often think that must be the kind of thing we will experience in heaven. People frequently comment that they want to be reunited with loved ones who have gone on before them. That is totally understandable, since almost all of us have had a deep, deep love for a least one person, and usually many more, here in the purple wedge and even back in the red circle. The best times we've had on earth are usually with those we love.

I mentioned earlier that there are many things I would do differently from the way God does things. Apparently I'm not alone, because many people say that when they get to heaven, they will be anxious to ask God questions about why He allowed something to happen or worked in some certain way. I've heard a few people say they can't wait to see their long-lost family pet. And with some people it's hard to tell whether they're serious or not when they say they can't wait to play heaven's perfect golf courses or make similar statements.

When people die, it's not so much that they have "died." Actually, it's more like that part of them that is alive, inside their shell of a body, moves to a different location. As mentioned before, Jesus told the thief on the cross, "I tell you the truth, today you will be with me in paradise" (Luke 23:43). That thief's body remained on earth, and its elements still do. Yet the part of him that was alive, and still is, went into the presence of God that very day. Paul must have been very aware of the joy and majesty to come in the blue kingdom as he spoke of whether he'd rather be in the purple wedge or the blue kingdom. He wrote, "We are confident, I say, and would prefer to be away from the body and at home with the Lord" (2 Corinthians 5:8).

So, should we all be drumming our fingers, waiting to get to the glories that await Christians when we die physically? Or worse yet, should we be considering suicide? Absolutely not, for as Paul pointed out in the very next verse, "So we make it our goal to please Him, whether we are at home in the body or away from it" (2 Corinthians 5:9). God's plan is better than our own. If you are a believer, consider it a tremendous gift that you have been given even the tiniest hints of how spectacular life in the blue kingdom will be.

To be present with the Lord undoubtedly will be overwhelming. In fact, it will be the most over-whelming thing we've ever experienced. Let's look at another biblical example.

The book of Revelation is interesting in that it is scary to some people yet intensely interesting to so many others who are curious about what will happen in the end times. Yet, it is in Revelation that we get a magnificent look at heaven and what goes on there. In Revelation, you'll find that the scene keeps bouncing back and forth from what is happening on earth, the red circle, to what is happening in heaven, the blue kingdom. I'll let you look to other authors for commentary on the earthly happenings. I invite you to read for yourself the scenes of heaven and what is happening there.

You will find, in a nutshell, that everyone in heaven is worshipping and praising God, in His presence, continually. Nowhere will you read about people looking for their long lost pets, asking God lists of questions from their note-pads, golfing, or even looking for those persons they loved more than anything else in life. Why?

Because they are so totally overwhelmed with being face to face with God in all His goodness and perfection. All they want to do is give themselves to Him. That's how great our God is! They have the intense desire to honor Him and nothing else. That's the way it was supposed to be on earth. Instead, sin turned it into "this world," the red circle.

I know a parent who explained all this to her little boy when he asked what heaven was like. His response was, "Sounds boring to me!" In some ways that is funny, but in another, I think it shows how blind all of us are to the overwhelming goodness and radiance of God. I am sure that the ruler of this world is thrilled and very proud of that.

I love reading in Revelation 21: 4 that "He will wipe away every tear from their eyes. There will be no more death and mourning or crying or pain, for the old things [the red-circle things] have passed away." I'm tired of seeing people hurting and crying. I've shed my own share of tears, and I'm sure you have too. I've experienced the hurt and sick feeling that comes with deaths and mourning, and I know you have too. We've all had physical and emotional pains, and sometimes they're excruciating. I just want all that stuff to go away, and I'll bet you do too. It will go away, for it will be absent in the blue kingdom. Meanwhile, here in the purple wedge, we are to "give thanks in all circumstances, for this is God's will for you in Christ Jesus" (1 Thessalonians 5:18). That's not easy to do, and this world will tell you it is stupid—and so are you for believing it. Like I said, if I were God, I probably wouldn't do it that way. In fact, I know I wouldn't. However, I surrender that arrogant attitude and bow down before Him, just like they're doing in those heavenly chapters of Revelation.

The blue kingdom sounds pretty good, doesn't it? It sounds especially good when you understand that it lasts forever. Consider this: you now live where God put you, in the gateway to that blue, perfect kingdom. It is next on your map. Your "you are here" mark is in that purple wedge on your map. Look back at where you've been. Look ahead to where you are going. It's as though the mall spent a fortune on backlighting on their directory map, and it couldn't be more clear! What a gift from God!

Chapter 12

THE BATTLE WITHIN

L et me address specifically those of you who are believers, and thus living in the purple wedge. Perhaps the biggest challenge of purple-wedge living is the fight the red puts up against the blue. And where is the battlefield? It's not only in the world; it's also in you! In your life there is a battle within. Many of you know it well. For others, this may be a wake-up call as to why there is such a push and pull in your life.

Before you were a believer, you were indoctrinated into the red circle in absolutely every way of your life. The focal point of that life was you. You learned it. You lived it. You got good at a bad way of life. When you became a Christian, you were still susceptible to living the way you learned to live before. Your brain was not wiped clean. That conflicts with this new life to which you gave yourself. Is it easy being a Christian in this world today? No! You are living in two contrary worlds at the same time. The two worlds have collided!

Many of the best and most admired Christian saints who have walked the face of the earth have admitted to, and agonized over, this battle in their purple wedge. Even while in the purple wedge, that little red circle pounds on us. In fact, it may hammer on us harder than it did before we became Christians. Earlier I listed some dilemmas of the purple wedge, and I mentioned then Paul's battle within described in Romans 7. As great as he was, Paul was not beyond living for himself. I have no idea what his particular weakness was that he hated so much, but he tells us he had at least one. Apparently he looked back at the red circle and saw something there he wanted, and he went after it. He chose Himself over God. Adam and Eve did that too in the Garden of Eden. I don't write about this so that we can gloat about how much better we are then they were. Quite the contrary! The whole point is that we are in exactly the same situation they were, and you and I both know that we frequently make bad decisions, just as they did. Overall, from the purple wedge, Paul looked toward the blue. He hated it when he looked back and grabbed into that old red garbage he'd already lived through. We should learn from his experience. As much as we don't want something to happen, on occasion we may lose a particular battle within. As we Christians strive to be more influenced by God's kingdom than by this world, we're reminded we will sometimes slip, but "if we confess our sins, he is faithful and just and will forgive our sins and purify us from all unrighteousness" (1 John 1: 9).

When you feel the battle within, look at your map and understand what is happening to you. Know that these things are going to present themselves to you. Don't be a bit surprised. Be ready. I once heard someone give a good analogy for falling into sin and then fleeing from it: "A bird may land on your head. That's his doing. But if he builds a nest in your hair, that's yours!"

Chapter 13

WHAT IF I DON'T BELIEVE?

One of the main reasons I wrote this book is because I saw so many Christians who, even though they were living in the purple wedge, seemed to continue to live as though they were totally in the little red circle, with no purple at all. I wanted to present this map so they could see, graphically, where they are, where they are going, and how futile it is to wallow in red-circle living like so many do, especially when they have received the greatest gift possible: salvation.

But I also know that some who are reading this book are not believers, and they are wondering where they show up on the map. Remember the little red circle. That is the world of the nonbeliever. On the left side is the day you were born. On the right side is the day you will die. Many nonbelievers seem to be OK with that, but that doesn't address what comes after the far right side of the red circle. Many nonbelievers think nothing does. I've not intended this to be a judgmental book or chapter, and I've already mentioned several times that if I were God I would do a number of things differently than He does. He says those who do not come to Him through His Son will be separated from Him forever. Eternal separation from God is the definition of hell. Many people in this world today want nothing to do with God, and God forces Himself on no one. The sad news from the Bible is that those who want nothing to do with God will get their way, not only now in this world, but also in eternity.

If you are not a believer, I want you to remember that I've written many times about how rough, hurtful, evil, and unfair this world, the red circle, is. I've even quoted Jesus and Paul with regard to how evil it is. As powerful as Jesus is, and after what human beings put Him through on earth, you would think God would just want to blow up the whole planet. Yet, amazingly, John

3:16 has something almost unbelievable to say about this world, the red circle.

> For God so loved *the world*, that he
> gave his one and only Son, that who-
> ever believes in him shall not perish,
> but have everlasting life.
> John 3:16

Jesus also declared, "I am the way, the truth and the life. No one comes to the Father but by me" (John 14:6).

Yes, you were born on the left side of the little red circle. I pray that you would present yourself to God through His Son. If you do, He will give you a second day of birth—not a second time you have a birthday, but a second time you are born! I pray you will be born again and thus enter that purple wedge. Jesus is the left boundary of that purple wedge. He is the only way to enter into it. Whether you realize it or not, it was a joyous day when you were born on the left side of the red circle, but even the angels themselves will celebrate your second birthday! Jesus said, "I tell you that in the same way there will be more rejoicing in heaven over one sinner that repents than over ninety-nine righteous persons who do not need to repent" (Luke 15:7).

Chances are I will never meet you, but if I could, it would be my heavenly honor to wish you a happy second birthday!

Chapter 14

SO WHAT? APPLICATION

N ow let's get really honest and practical. So what if I lived in a small red circle called "this world," had God's kingdom come into my life, putting me in the purple wedge, and will eventually pass into the 100 percent "blueness" of that kingdom? It makes for an interesting story and diagram, but how does that change anything for you and me right here, right now? So what?

If you bought a brand-new hammer and never used it, it's actually as if you never bought it at all. No matter how many nails need to be hammered, the hammer makes absolutely no difference. You bought a hammer; so what? Whatever you do with what you read and experience in this book, I beg you, DON'T DO NOTHING!

My biggest joy from all this has been a total change in the way I see and handle frustrations, troubles, sorrows, disappointments, unfairness, trials, problems, and even things as deep as depression and devastation. I often saw and felt each one of these from a totally "red-circle, this-world" point of view. I had my share of pity parties, and from a worldly point of view, most of them were justified. But no matter how justified I thought they were, that didn't make the circumstances go away. "In this world you will have trouble," Jesus honestly warned us (John 16:33).

Many people waiting for true happiness are waiting for things to go extraordinarily well for them in the red circle. Many of them have found this to be a long, disappointing wait. Although we have happy moments, the cares and trials of this world frequently overwhelm the hope that there will be true, unending happiness in our lives, and it saddens us. Whether you're a Christian or a nonbeliever, if you are waiting for the red circle to make you happy, you will die waiting.

We are incapable of making many circumstances go away, but we can take our life and those circumstances and fit them into our map. Any person, at any age, in any walk of life, at any time can use this map to his or her advantage. That's something that makes this book unique. It seems as though everybody is writing a book. My goal and prayer was that, through God, I could write a book for everybody. The president of the United States can apply this book to his life as he looks at it in the Oval Office. So can a homeless person looking at it while living under a bridge. The lives of nurses, teachers, welders, pastors, teenagers, moms, dads, homemakers, insurance agents, auto mechanics, husbands, wives, web designers, sales people, policemen, baristas, and on and on fit on this map. Not only can everyone use it, but also everyone can use it every moment of every day for the rest of his or her life!

By all means, save this book. Get it out frequently! New challenges, disappointments, and trials will undoubtedly come your way. The map will apply when you have different circumstances later on, maybe even tomorrow. Just pay special attention to when those things are red-circle trials, and keep looking toward the blue, knowing that you are already in that blue kingdom, even though the red world is staining that blue into the purple in which you live.

The first time I said anything about any of this purple wedge stuff to anyone was when I was in the hospital room of a Christian friend who had just days to live. I had no intention of getting into it, because the idea was fairly new to me and I wasn't sure I had it down correctly in my own mind. The next thing I knew, I had a piece of scrap paper and was drawing it out for him, explaining it. He looked at me with tears in his eyes and yet with a huge smile and said, "That is exactly what I needed to see, and it gives me incredible peace. Thank you." I knew that God did that, and I wondered if it could help others.

For me the most immediate gratification came when I looked back at the red circle, especially the left side of it, and saw what it was and where I had been. So many of my past problems and challenges were red-circle/earthly disappointments. The more I dwelled on them, the more depressing it got. I had treated my temporary earthly problems so emotionally and seriously that they became major energy zappers, brain drains, and heart breakers. I knew I was a Christian living in this world, but things didn't really sink in until the concept of the purple wedge made me "see" it and put things into perspective.

This world dishes up a lot of garbage. That is what I was looking at and upon which I focused. I know many others who are doing the same thing. On the map, that garbage reveals itself as worldly, nagging, but evaporating events and emotions. To the right is the big, blue, never-ending kingdom of God. Now the question for believers is this: What will you do and how will you act in that purple wedge between the little red circle and the huge, blue kingdom? Will you live just as you did when you were totally in the red circle, letting it dominate, control and frustrate you? Or will you focus on the right side of the map? Will you focus on the muck of where you've been or the unbelievable, never-ending glory of where you are going? Remember, as a believer, you are already in God's kingdom, even if you are still standing on this earth.

Now that I can picture this, so what? Personally I'm choosing to dwell upon the glory of the kingdom of which I am a part, even though I'm still a witness and sometimes a victim of the junk in "this" world. Just in the last few hours while writing this book, I have had some terrible distractions, disappointments, and concerns come my way from the world. They interrupted my writing—or tried to. They were distressing, and my knee-jerk reaction was to be upset by them. The next reaction came from inside: "Hey, Van, are you going to live what you are writing?" I plowed through, finished up, sat back in the chair, and basked in how much more important this work was than the earthly disappointments that wanted my full attention. Was I thrilled with the worldly things going on? No. Did I have a bit of a pit in my stomach? Yes. In all honesty, if I had not been writing on this topic, perhaps I would have taken some time out for another one of those pity parties. I didn't. I pressed on. This kind of thing is easier said than done. You cannot do it on your own. Let God do it through you!

Bask in the good news that is in this book. Be ready for distractions and disappointments. How will your mood and attitude change when you hit those struggles? You may very well be knocked off track for a while. But now you have the ammunition to fire back at this world by knowing how all these things fit in with everything else in your life. Enjoy the perspective, and best wishes to you on your journey!

Chapter 15

IN CONCLUSION: THE LORD'S PRAYER IN RED, PURPLE, AND BLUE

OUR FATHER

Dear Creator of everything, including all of us, I call out to you.

WHICH ART IN HEAVEN

You are in Your 100 percent blue, perfect kingdom.

HALLOWED BE THY NAME.

Of the millions of names in any world—red, purple, or blue—none come close to Yours. You created everything and are above us all, far above the highest of high in this red circle of earth.

THY KINGDOM COME.

May Your blue kingdom come to take over and even eliminate the red kingdom of this world.

THY WILL BE DONE ON EARTH, AS IT IS IN HEAVEN.

And when Your kingdom does come, may the perfection of what You want replace the imperfection of what we, often-selfish, humans want. Make it here like You make it in your 100 percent blue kingdom.

GIVE US THIS DAY OUR DAILY BREAD.

Anything and everything I need comes from You. Please continue to provide for me as You see fit.

AND FORGIVE US OUR DEBTS [TRESPASSES],

I do and think things I shouldn't. I'm truly sorry. Life is difficult in the red circle, and even in this purple wedge, sin creeps in on me. You are so much more important than that garbage, and I know that only You can forgive me. I don't deserve it because of anything I have done. Thank You for doing it through Your Son and what He has done.

AS WE FORGIVE OUR DEBTORS [THOSE WHO TRESPASS AGAINST US].

You've made it clear that if I won't forgive someone in this world, I will not receive forgiveness myself. That is very hard in the evil of this red-circle world, but I know what You say is true; so I ask You to flow Your forgiveness through me. I may not be able to do it in my power, but I can do all things through You.

AND LEAD US NOT INTO TEMPTATION,

Please steer me away from the evil hooks and dangling bait of this world.

BUT DELIVER US FROM EVIL:

In this purple wedge in which I live, keep my eyes, heart, and mind always looking to the right of the map, to Your blue Kingdom. Pull me that way. I've already been in the red of this evil world, and I need not go back. Once was enough.

FOR THINE IS THE KINGDOM,

Yours is the never-ending blue kingdom of perfection. There is no other true kingdom.

AND THE POWER,

You are the only true, perfect power anywhere. To stray from that is foolishness.

AND THE GLORY,

I've looked so many places for glory and happiness. Thank you for being patient with me and teaching me that You, and only You, are the source of both.

FOR EVER.

And nothing will ever change that, ever!

AMEN.

Matthew 6:9-13 (KJV)

CPSIA information can be obtained at www.ICGtesting.com
Printed in the USA
LVOW01s1600020414

379999LV00001B/1/P